Praise for *a tender force:*

"Each poem in this collection is an exquisite and well-crafted facet of life. They reveal moments of clarity and mindfulness, insight into encounters with hard truths, disappointments, happiness, yearnings of the heart, tender and sometimes fleeting moments of love and connection, death and more. There is much wisdom to be found here."

Sharon Salzberg, author of *Lovingkindness* and *Real Happiness*

"This delightful and thought-provoking collection of brief poetical reflections evokes a sense of mindful experience of living, sharing, feeling, being. There is wise perspective offered of subtle elements of life that may grab our attention, but deserve our deeper awareness. *a tender force* is likely to draw you into creating that deeper awareness within your own life."

Jean Kristeller, Ph.D., mindfulness practitioner, scientist, and teacher

"Melissa Joseph's poems are good company. I identify with her world which makes me more aware of mine. She is a poet of wisdom; her language and vision are refreshing in their simplicity and clarity."

Mary Kay Gardner, author of the poetry collection *Captured Moments*

"Melissa Joseph's a *tender force* is a luxuriant and insightful collection of poems. In her delicately sparse but supple verses, Joseph transports us to an entrancing and yet evanescent place beyond words. We are gifted a glimpse into this thoughtful and sincere trove of tenderness and force, enough to knock us off our ordinary perceptions into something much more meaningful."

Cherie Kephart, award winning author of *A Few Minor Adjustments: A Memoir of Healing and Poetry of Peace*

"I am drawn to the contemporary and truthful voice of Melissa Joseph. Her poems possess sensuality, passionate energy, a self-searching loneliness and romantic new age encounters as she searches for lightness and connections with others. Her detailed observations are articulate. *a tender force* is a compelling journey into Melissa's contemporary world."

Seretta Martin, poet, editor, teacher, publisher and managing editor of the *San Diego Poetry Annual.*

"*a tender force* is a collection of short juicy stories, coded in poetry that evokes our own mental illustrations. You'll find your own questions about relationships, sexuality, technology, intimacy, sanity and your own mental voices wrapped in evocative images. A journey to evoke, enjoy and share, thanks to Melissa Joseph."

Pamela Hale, award-winning author, spiritual mentor and artist

a tender force

melissa joseph

KONSTELLATION
PRESS

Published by
Konstellation Press, San Diego
Copyright © 2018 Melissa Joseph
Cover design: Max Feye
Illustrations: Irina Gronborg
Melissa portrait photo: Holly Rone
All rights reserved.
ISBN: 0998748293
ISBN-13: 9780998748290

DEDICATION

to all those individuals who are on a quest to know
the truth, become their
highest self, and demonstrate concern for others.

and to my faithful pal, Lotus,
who teaches me that time is only now, love is all there
is, and being playful
matters.

CONTENTS

TENDERNESS

love

not a feeling

nor a thought

a tender force

of the heart

CONNECTIONS

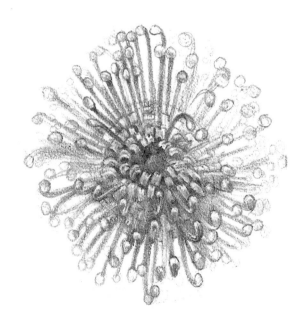

soul mates

two women

meet later in life

yep online

match.com

back n' forth

maybe

maybe not

it becomes yes

one moves

to the other's

they're knitted

no one else required

the fabric

not synthetic

maybe cashmere

with many pockets

a handsome wrap

indeed

there's only one

they both wear it

she's the front

with the pockets

the other the back

with the pleat

the one

with the pockets

reaches for the other

places her hand inside

they are interchangeable

both hands in one pocket

the crying heart

i hold myself

wanting you to hold me

instead no one is there

my arthritic knobby hands

feel me up

wondering what you would feel

but you're not here

i open my legs

and rub inside that space

tears glaze over

i see only darkness

i hold my hand

with my other hand

i'd rather your hand

be the other hand

but you haven't

come to me

yet

madame jackie

she's a tarot card reader

pulling up to her desk

an imaginary turban

adorns her crown

i see jewels that were hidden

for me to recognize

pouring from a suede bag

she lays out nonchalantly a shiny pile

pretty polished small rocks

she chooses some

and I choose mine

motivated by size color

hers I don't know

maybe these are telling gems

if i choose wisely

or is it just in the stars

does she have telepathic energies

forces that allow her

to tap into an unknown

inside me

i am open to

the power

that makes all credible

to entertain as possible

she knows facts about me

i confess nothing

she reads me raw

sees me right

i leave

buoyant

not from her details

instead

the truth

crystal

tucked in an envelope
on a post-it note
coy is scribbled
to remind me of you

was our kiss
as intoxicating
as that blackberry cooler
you had earlier
almost oozing
down your spine

did the diaphanous lamp shade
distract you from holding my hand
your topaz eyes emitted a glitter
to seal that envelope

just to remember
why i met you

meeting gary

he sent me a photo

to recognize him

at track 9

in union station

astonished

he was that picture

ironically

he wasn't that mug shot

he was so much more

william

his head

a light bulb

never flickering

on

to where

you can hear him buzz

neither yale nor harvard

nope he came up

from his own two feet

pressing hard

toes grabbing the soil

turning it over

planting a thought

which grew

into

preternatural

wisdom

claudia

is it possible to hear you
with my ears folded over
i make little room
to hear your voice

even in your silence
i bury myself
in my own soliloquy

i continue on the trail
my relentless noise
disappears for you

as you grasp the ground
with your soles
you feel the reverberation
that matches your own

with your gemstone intellect
you search for a place to hide
to rest your sweet spirit
finally to be alone

you show me
the value
to be quiet

in the audible
utter silence
of the forest

meeting jane hirshfield

i'm neither thief nor coveter of you
yet i want to fondle your words

dress them up as my own
saturate in their
evocativeness

i drink your tears
to taste
heartache and joy

this begins and ends
on your exquisite paper

where i take your words
to wrap my wound

DISCONNECTION

ephemeral cloud

i'm not consciously excited

nor creating false vignettes

just floating landing

taking off

all seems ethereal

maybe i'm hallucinating

none of this is real

though it seems true

like a cloud occurs

amorphous then moves on

and you

exist from afar

i do not back up my words

nor delete them

i hit send

syllables are not returned

no person there

i can neither taste

nor smell you

see or touch you

 i am a mystery to you

which keeps the fire hot

no embers in sight

please fan away

seduce me wet

until tomorrow

i can't find

the match

to light

what remains

plastic surgery

thighs

lipo'd

lips

puffed

face

unwrinkled

lids

raised

make

yourself

perfect

dress

your

heart

in love

acceptance

wrap in a vow

of unbreakable honesty

to heal

broken hearts

nyc

any combination is possible
imaginable or not
no juxtaposition is excluded
full of surprises

sometimes turns into a trend
others disappear into the streets
the infinity of choice
gives way to acceptance

most ethnicities there
under those skyscrapers
living with their histories
explained on their faces

there is no benchmark
for pain greed or joy
in the cab
on the train

intoxicating
refreshing
alive
perfect

grunge

the subway

a certain reputation

people ignore

their destinations

my eyes

no direct contact

just to the sign

the man i can't recall

help

my family

was killed

by aliens

i think the sign hilarious

how repugnant of me

dispassionate

callous

people

like him

everywhere

why do we argue

over

the truth

why would anyone tamper

with facts

such as this disheveled man

begging for aid

maddening

knocking and knocking
talking over each other
the bell rings non-stop
why do all these people
want to come inside me

telling me this, arranging that
story after story
and made up ones too

would you please go away
you're not invited to my cranium
this is not reasonable
for you to continuously show up

do you ever consider this rude
are you that recalcitrant
that you won't listen
to my telling you to stop

you go on for hours on end

awakening me in the middle of the night

don't you ever go to sleep yourself

are you mad or just mean spirited

i'm going to ask you nicely

leave me the fuck alone

forever

sour milk

you're there

so far away

i'm spilled milk

running down the container

can't wipe it up

it will smell soon

help

breath

sourness

like a lemon

discarded into an ashtray

is still there

in the sunlit hours

before dawn

i'm up

the immaculate hour

soundless

of man

resplendent

of nature

trees breathe

their fog

wetting others

the roots

hold hands

several times

he reaches for mine

the third time

i hold his

awkwardly

haphazardly

unmethodically

only feeling wrong

unidentifiable

still

it's another's suffering

where we can merge

enough to kiss goodbye

that's when i got the waft

unimaginable

his lips were trying

to purse

never

ever

will i go inside

distracted

there's no new insight

just a take on some aphorism

before you were born

the truth has always been

the truth

twittering

not even

a cogent thought

not a thought at all

just busy

disturbed

plastic ugly smoke detector

screwed to a wall

directions not to paint

i threaten it with metallic silver

expressly it goes off and on

a piercing cacophony

disturbing my dog

in the middle of the night

awakening her from an audible snore

to panting frantic pacing wildness

she wants to flee

take her paws

and cover her ears

but she can't

she's stuck in the din

like chalk screeching down a board

the noise makes her mad

unsettled unfocused unhinged

i rip out the battery

it continues to emit a toxic sharp beep

using a screw driver to tear out another

i gash my finger

trailing blood on all I touch

i resort to scissors

slicing the wires

before the last sound

makes a hole in my heart

tech romance

off the path

untraveled

a hidden café

unaware to tourists

mesmerizing

like a man on his knees

pleading his love devotion

the couple comfortably ensconced

en face

on their phones

the quotidian marriage

he was a porky guy
dressed in a plaid summer shirt
maybe a tourist's disposition
she frumpy twirling her bad hair color blonde
staring at him glaring as his phone
texting away
she was waiting for lunch
he for a reply

just a typical day
in their dissatisfying marriage
decades in the same bed
never sharing a dream
or fondling under the covers
neither showering under the same head
nor backing up to mildewed wall
holding one another

space between them
now the phone
connects him
at last to something
other than her

touch

those blasted blowers

where's the broom

being in touch

with body and earth

and the darned hair dryer zooms

where's the towel and sun

the electric razor

something in between

hand to skin

and the letter

really

i need a stamp

oh just text

i had a really nice time

thank you

the din of silence

the refrigerator box emits energy
the heat vibrates the corner
and pieces of crust rest below

the clock sends a spark of light
across the ceiling
coaxing me to turn my head
to see it's neither morning
nor night

it's the time when most sleep
except for those restless minds
and dying souls
who reach for that glow
which grabs them
and takes them away
from the cacophony of life
into the place of nothing
or everything

the address i fear

the end of what i think i know

and the beginning of what

i know i don't

inside out

soothe the outside

spa luxuriate

someone to dote over you

pay handsomely

for those hands

to touch you

in exterior places

while the interior

remains fraught with you

the part that needs

those hands

delving into your spirit

massaging your soul

bringing you to life

making all sanguine

just as it is on the outside

no need for that $100 jar

of magic cream

there is neither magic

nor replacement

for digging in the trenches

of soggy muck where goblins bathe

and angels are repulsed

some place in between

you reside

in the warmth of the earth

and the light of the moon

.

SENSUALITY

making love

it's been a long time

more than a week

i confess

like months

count all my toes

and fingers

times three years

today

no formal invite

at random

it came to me

not a person

nor a bedroom

not even an image

it was an unveiling

before my eyes

whose weight

pushed open

my heart

a disappearing door
offered an opening
a capacious
space

oozing of crystal waters
covered in clarity

i know this
there before
here now
never gone

love making

teeter-totter

that feeling comes roiling in
it's clear and then like the marine layer
it's eerie hue portending darkness
all possibility of joy evaporates

just as that sepia sky
will open its arms to brightness
each day goes somewhat like this
back n' forth

the prism so dense
i can't break out
then an event
turns me around

there i am once again
somewhere to be found

you take me from behind
burying your chest
into the back of my heart

i place my hand

over your warm shoulder

and in these moments

the madness i witnessed

is now merely a nightmare

in passing

like love when it reaches the other

and you then part ways

remembering it was a dream

patchwork life

begins with mandarin orange

melding into cheap nail polish fuchsia

changing to salmon pink

clashing hard against ink marker red

penetrating to a cloud of sky grey

then to a bluish mood and enviable green

making exotic larimar aqua

falling abruptly

into rusted steel

mixing with

burnt black

awakening

to uplifting

daffodil yellow

in full bloom

of renewal

whole flesh

since i now have myself

i would like to jump

inside of you

have you

love me

and

i will still

remain

myself

awake

if love is all that matters

then serve me platters

feast for your sustenance

that will expand your heart

enhance yourself

relinquishing your trance

lessen your suffering

distract you from ego

and always take you

home

nowhere else to go

there's no better entree

condiment or appetizer to say

you will be satiated

even in your last breath

pure elation

never placation

lobster mushroom

musty spaces

like looking through

the crook of an elbow

and the sleeve

crumpled, folded

not pressed

cotton-like fragile

pithy and chewy

she answers a one line question

with lobster mushroom indentions

where you're left with your palette

full of swirling flavors

an underbelly

that needs a scrub to decipher

lobster mushroom so much more

even for the unblurred eye

leaf

the sway of the mind

with a blustering sharp branch in my face

i fall to the earth

cool, dank surface

i am still alive

uninjured

jolted by the force

there's a slit over my lip

blood is on my tongue

i taste it

begin to talk to myself

why are there so many leaves

i just want to examine one

feel its bumpy veins

view its dying hues

and smell the musty earth

from whence it came

the tree where it was left for dead

and the leaves to be trampled

or pressed onto wax paper

to be admired and identified

completely unique

birds

you can't hear their voice

unless you stop

and listen

blue

the shiny penny inserted in his loafer

took me to his feet

one blue sock the other unmatched

as my head dangled against his epaulet

the blues grabbed my weakened heart

my friend brought me a vase of blue delphiniums

i set them on the back of the toilet

to see happiness

while i threw up from the cancer drugs

i looked in the mirror to find the spots to clean

and there my cheeks were sunken in

with a blue tinged shadow

the disease had depressed my desert skin

the stronghold made me shiver

and my toes were bluish from little blood

my veins matched

as my feet were a pair

the window behind the flowers
shone the blue cloud infused sky
as i clawed the muted blue shag carpet
infested with loose strewn hair

my life was arriving at a new destination
i grabbed for my favorite pen
the lawyer said i must use blue ink
to sign my will

white

like baking soda

clean and pure

i noticed it

first light

yesterday closed

and colored magenta

today

white

a flower from my cactus

immersing from bruised arms

sore spots

indentions

on your face

you call them wrinkles

you would botox

undo mother nature

reverse time

change your age

here the soul remains

embedded in soil

grounded

beautiful as is

accept it all

this is you

delight

the heater is toasty

while the clouds

turn into stars

the delicate fish

is on my plate

it was swimming earlier

now dead

the dry spell

the santa ana winds

inhale dry all moisture

stealing from flowers

the roots of trees

the person

who swears off drink

to feel all feelings

in deprivation

the poet

who longs for words

dried up

inside some broken pen

looking for sustenance

maybe a glass of water

hoping to find tears

to feel any feelings

salty essentials

the table

holds the shaker

salt

the ocean

invisible salt

left on your skin

sore throat

gargle

salt

water

stir

scrubs

add salt

oils

mix

recipes

a pinch of

salt

the body

requires

salt

heat

sweat

taste salt

for life

salt

NaCl

juicy fruit

robbed of the essence

of eating fruit

how clever

to entice you

with the fake

you deem real

though sinister

insidious

addictive

draws you in

to rot your teeth

spasm your jaw

taint your palate

whoa the essence

of mother nature's bounty

versus the concoctions of humans

her bounty

his juicy fruit

DOUBT

the if game

what if no one ever reads this

what if these words are merely

vowels and consonants

on a white page

that no one turns to the next

what if i was inspired

and found a vocabulary

to sound my tune

and it resonated

with no one

not even you

who am i

if i'm not my body

or my thoughts

nor my feelings

who and what

am i

a beating heart

longing

to hear the sound

just is

anyone could write

these very same words

the vocabulary requires

no page turn of the oxford

.

though cryptic at times

housed in metaphor illusions innuendos

personal if you will

tragic and humorous

the fact of the matter

they didn't

i did

it just is

let's say

air is free

unless you pollute

then a tax is imposed

plastic bags

cost ten dollars

bad food

costs twice

zero emissions

a monthly bonus

maintain a healthy weight

no medications

free health care

no deductions

no exceptions

water recycled

free water

you pay

you destroy

you save

you preserve

reward good choices

penalize destructive ones

you contribute to

or start a green company

education is free

you give back

you receive kick back

let's say

you have choice

in this free world

what if

the game

of creating

your future

recreating

your past

making

a new reality

to further

untruths

the toxic game

distracts

disarms

deludes

destroys

entangles

you

you have

many players

death

not one

it cannot play

death is real

the casket

dressed up

in your finest fare

shoes that shine

and make up

glitters

neither a pimple

nor a wrinkle

dry cleaner

pressed

snugged into place

a perfect fit

just your size

all ready you are

for a barney's window

funny

you're not

headed for nyc

the ground

your destination

frozen, chilly in winter

include a coat please

sweaty in summer

beach wear instead

with sunscreen haha

the ideal time

fall with the burnt leaves

spring with the freshest bloom

when will you go

all i'm saying

have them

dress you

correctly

you do want to remain

at ease

bon voyage

elimination

if i eliminate

that ugly old place within

i will be free

yet it is still with me

neither escape nor annihilation

will kill its soul

it must live

a part of me

like the energy

of creation

or matter

lay it aside

in truth you abide

to recognize

no longer hide

you embrace

that and this

you are the jury

the shaman

the healer

you are the way

only you

can find you

no amount

of therapy

drugs

sex

or love

from another

you must fall

for yourself

in every way

not be taller

than you are

uncover your style

not beneath the magazine cover

nor a TV screen

or a cell phone

instagram

you create you

your own unique self

not to be defended

to be lived worn torn

broken in

comfortable

at ease and satisfied

what you search

your desk is an infinity pool

papers drowning over the edge

smothered beneath the cold

others strewn on the uncarpeted floor

to slip beneath your feet

and you can't find

that one something

among all the white pages

either there or here

clear the detritus

what you search

you already hold

alone

how alone am i
i can feel my breath
and my body
that i'm alive

i see the trees
grounded to the earth
the flower blossoms
married to their stem

there are neighbors
appointments to keep
the person on the phone
my dog still asleep

the ticket to see a distant friend
future plans to be with others
ideas to explore the world
to meet people like me
who live alone
but aren't alone

ALONE with the ALONE

is death the reason

to contemplate

knowing all along

it will end

the only thing

one knows

is life an opportunity

to touch a soul

in order

to wake up your own

are the daily comings and goings

a reason to exist

is that meaningful

another night darkens the bedroom

assuming light will arrive after

you rest like a corpse

and by random chance

you die

and what is your life

years that you counted

to celebrate what occasion

that the number

will go on to infinity

meditation

in the midst of the matter
if and it's a
colossal if

you could take me
and know what to do
as they say
have your way

we could move through
maybe not soar
float over the stalagmites
not getting scathed this time

take a deep breath
without thought
no feelings to conjure
or over which to ruminate
neither reflect nor interpret

instead with the force
of a power that is sure
a touch that's familiar

not from over and over

but experience

real

from a previous time

that was appropriate

with that age

which brought us

to this day

to this time

to today

but it didn't happen

no dreamland

came true

SENSIBILITY

five syllable word

if love

were a five syllable word

i'd marry it

if love weren't silent

what would it say

if it were colorful

what arc of a rainbow

if it had ears

how would you hear it

and eyes

how would you view it

not with your ego

only your heart

undefended

unattached

untethered

broken bent twisted

and well formed

love is not a thought

to be analyzed

a sensibility

a resonance

a timbre that rings

through and through

idyllic

for love to be held

it must remain infinitesimal

conditions can reside

through

and around

love can neither

die nor hide

definition

what do you call

the space

in between

an open eye

and a blink

yoga

when i come to my mat
i begin again
with the reminder
of a beginner's mind

my body stuck
as if it's never seen a mat
much less sat there
done a pose

cross legged in meditation
it's a new breath
my body
gets accustomed
all over again

how to move
unfurl
relax
let go

muscles tight

contracted

sore

something shifts

that new breath

becomes familiar

to my body

the sound

echoes anew

yesterday's situations

dissolve

the tomorrow to do list

unwritten

today

is this breath

the journal

one fourth of the journal's pages used
i thought of you with each opening
such a sweet gift

to esalen it accompanied me
close by
thought of you each time

and before that
all the way to costa rica
like a passport
i stamped it

moments into words
travails into expressions
ideas for resolve
i put down
on paper

to return
to remember what was

full moon

today

i become

tiny

unto myself

silent

turned inside out

like a post note

folded into its mini envelope

my organs are exposed

to the morning first light

to call forth the blood

the high sun

to soothe their cold

with the rain

to relax

their pulsation

the afternoon arrives

holding dusk overhead

to rest their labors

and the full moon

a lamp to take them to bed

i unfold afterwards

the inside turns outside

i am released

wide awake

sound asleep

the mind

startles

a story

begins

a series

of little

vignettes

none true

like a

short story

one right

after

the

other

i'm not even turning a page

3 a.m.

clawing the sheets

wanting a stopper for my mind

and a soft pillow for my heart

to find the beauty

that i'm still alive

i'm here

and there

is another land

with sounds of galloping wild stallions

kicking up the desert dust

scratching the cactus

as they launch

into the wide open sky

that's where i want to go

with freedom for brothers and sisters

to make a family

of sentient beings

that all belong

right here

to hide

in the folds of my own skin
or the underbelly of my dog

up and awake
in between the furled fitted sheet
and the still warmed comforter

up and awake
in the middle of my last line read
the book of another person's story

up and awake
in that place
before the day begins

DARKNESS

tethered

the mollusk's tendrils

dug into my mind

pulling up stories

all attached

to a tangled time

examining the past

in the sleepless night

no way to see with crystal eyes

convoluted by years

buried on years of fright

i fought off his amorphous arms

as he grabbed the detritus inside

jettisoning the load to sea

he disappeared

carrying off my past

exhausted sleep takes over me

i awaken later from the

nightmare to see

suction marks dot my body

where i struggled

to untether myself

free

maurice

esther prynne with her scarlet a
the nazis with their insignia
jews with their arm band
many others had their mark
but my father
he held a torch for cruelty
not for himself

i recall no personal brow beating
only furrowing his towards those
for whom antipathy had no reason
it just was

and i was one of them
one of those people
chosen to be beaten down
then to receive a sliver of love
just to make sure
i'd come back for more

face it

i would sneak into my mom's jaundice yellow
bathroom
try on her sparse makeup selection
drugstore quality blush lipstick mascara

i thought it would make me look better happier
completely transform me
from ugly to pretty

my makeover changed nothing
my visage morphed
into a clown figure

i smeared off the new mask
scrubbed til raw my stained skin
yearning to rub me anew

there was no escape
redolent with shame
i left with my original self

the afghan

i used my mother's heirloom
to build
my private protected fort

i tucked the bulky end
into the top drawer
of my melamine built-in desk
the remainder heavily fell to the ground
creating complete darkness inside

when they yelled
and daddy threw furniture
or launched a pair of scissors at her
i hid
using the blanket as a wall
buffering me from them
and their scary sounds

i would keep the opaque sheath
even in waves of silent times
not knowing when the conflagration
would begin again

it was interminable

like cancer

and my sadness

with neither apology nor regret

daddy would afterwards flee

never peaking over his shoulder

he slammed the front door

it vibrated as forcefully

as my body heaved in tears

i wondered

who would come and stay with me

this time

mama was going away

i plodded up and down

the sketchy attic stairs

white knuckling her suitcase

stopping in between

hoping she would stay

i wanted to save her
for us to both jump inside
and leave together in her valise

i knew she would return
she adored me

the end

mama was dead

prostrate on her back

still adorned with her

lacy blush nightgown's yoke

poking out

from underneath aunt mattie's

home spun gangrene green afghan

splayed with a bold r for rosenfield

mama turned icy as time etched forward

as if the moving hands would catapult me

to a happier unmet future

i couldn't get separate

from my unstoppable grief

strangling me

like the weight of a man

i no longer loved

in the end

longing, madness, loneliness, love

which one becomes you

in this moment

how often

do you interchange one

unbeknownst

that you just did

robotic like

is your mind

a trickster

as your mood cycles

like coming down

from caffeine

then surging back up

with another cup

ride those waves

they never go away

there is a day

the illusion of a lake

a day to float

perhaps depression
looms over the top
like early morning fog
you can neither see through it
nor time its disappearance

can you control your mind
and witness those feelings
when they arise
as another loved one's death
supposedly wakes you up
to your own impermanence

maybe your birth
was the reincarnation
and the end
is the end

death

isn't death

only

a departure

from

the

body

until death do us part

it gnaws on me

like a lonely dog

with a bone

the buzzard

rips on my heart

as i bleed

it croons

you deserve

to disappear

i awaken

in the midst

of a symbolic death

i am born at last

to accept

who i am

INSIGHT

happiness recipe

heaping dollop of self-love

add 2 C full of gratitude

slowly whip in open slow

non-judgmental pourings

of love throughout the day

at the end

with purposeful deep inquiry

without judgment

taste the outcome

reflection

first light
i love myself

day time
i show love to others

stars
how well did I love today

random

nothing

that seems

random

is

random

there's a message

silence your phone

corral your thoughts

don't disturb yourself

listen

through

your

pores

to every nuance

that transpires

in your life

pay close attention

like skin to your bones

or you'll miss

your answer

that

becomes

wisdom

esalen (retreat)

lying on the floor
listening to a podcast

a bustling fire
in the black stove
stretching out
my older contracted self
from a day of travels

i peer up
through a large skylight
with large draping branches
painting the glass

i hear birds
see them flying
the branch right here
another branch there

they aren't in need of rescuing
nor suffering
they aren't thinking
they're flying

meditating

being

knowing

exactly how to live

the ocean blasts behind me

birds' songs above

inside me

a troubled noise

searching to harmonize

closing my eyes

i know

the bird's harp

the sea's cymbals

both exist

within me

re-entry from retreat

i must leave this womb

with folks whose hearts

beat with mine

and minds that listen

without petty internal remarks

to a world of cellular

flimsy handshakes

and conversations

interrupted by a text

i need to be some place else

right then

no fluidity

in the artificial world

where gluttony is a habit

and smiles exist

over a positive response

on facebook

and sadness comes

when one

is slightly delayed

it's a curious place
here
and there
where I was

call it
a kind
of home

the circle

did i form that circle

to keep you out

or keep me in

to let me be without

horde it all for myself

unable to share a morsel

able to see in

only one direction

all along thinking

a 360 degree view

because it's a circle

what if it were a line

a continuum of space

limitless timeless

undefinable

merely

beginnings

much in between

and endings

opening

the gate has no key

therefore no lock

not a clasp

for closing shut

it's revolving

taking you in

either direction

into yourself

outside your being

to become

curious

grit and grace

pull myself up

by tattered laces

worn running shoes

hour by hour

trudging my feet

in and down

sinking in muck

my story

the title

grit

cover myself up

in a velvet swathe

rise fiercely

with a rod like spine

each moment

gliding through silk

effortlessly settled

my story

the title

grace

the fulcrum

displeasure on one side
pleasure on the other

always there seems to be
one or the other

either way
there's a reaction
attached

a story develops
emotions take over

any situation
positive
negative

yet it's the middle
the center
where there's neither

that space

that's masked

as emptiness

is indeed

happiness

source

where does it sit

inside of me

does it have a bed

when is it hiding

silently

siri

exact location please

under my stomach

inside my right armpit

where my razor won't

reach

i know

i see

in the mirror

the small of my back

a spec there

sole of my left foot

palm of the hand

glared into

all those places

not there

you guessed

am i right

you're wise

and i forget

to remember

i'm wise too

i forget that

the paper slit

slithers in my

mindless voice

only to discover

the source is without word

nor thought

not place

love

mindless energy

the futon there

for the cacophony

to rest

if at all

the sword

without a double edge

the forever sharpened

sharpie

the inkless pen

the reams of paper

til infinity

burn it all

merge their power

emblazon everything

with love

even the raunchiest

most putrid smelling

tarry phlegm bile

say halt

to it all

the door

no bother to search

for the entrance

nor the exit

the adventure

is not in trying

it's simply allowing

openings

closings

and

all the space

in between

a zen moment

you feel your heart beat

reverberating

thru your entire body

harmonizing

with the pulse

of the universe

undisturbed by turbulence

calm in emptiness

elation

as it all turns into

equipoise

.

SUFFERING

torment

i long to get inside

the made up bed

neat and not fixed by me

it awaits me through the day

pillows fluffed up

smooth lines fresh

something rubs me

edges sting

corners sharp

against my skin

antagonistic

restless mind

bottle stated calm

effect a hallucinogen

swashing my brain

mixed colors

not a rainbow

clashing lights

thrashing

coddling in plastic

cold edgy unwelcoming

nowhere to crawl

911 seems possible

sleep not

reaching inside my gown

my heart grabs me

in sync with my pulse

is my heart under attack

breathe into my third eye

my fingers apply pressure

on my stomach

i retreat into blackness

the beat subsides

it's now time

i unfurl

to tell this

oh no

i've run out of bandaids
steri strips, paper tape
duct tape super glue

i'm squashed
the size of my body
bent over my knees
draping to touch
the earth's surface

no more places to fold up
there's soiled laundry
to come clean

i might as well
expose my wound
and allow
it to dissolve

permanent injury

go away

you bring me grief

yet maybe just maybe

you are what i reap

a reminder of the limitation

or better still

a punctuation of infinity

instead of an attachment

to insanity

affording an ability

a capacity to stop and see

to open the gerbil cage door

release the need to spin

settle into this nest of self

and be more than that pain

which is only a reminder

of what was

not what is

BECOMING

numbers

my single digit days are long over

and soon the double ones will end

it will come as surprise to some

to others it will be as common

and natural as a dog

ambling to the woods

to bury into the musky earth

into the massive arms of mother nature

dies peacefully silently without

fuss or muss

a whimper into the paw

only a leash and collar to dispose

such a simple way to go

hope

the conflagration inside

the crash of the rolling waves

the silence of the sand

under your feet

the milky brown foam

spreading over your toes

like an old man drooling

over his bib

child like

in the nursing home cafeteria

you wait

not for that day

for hope

cinching it up

like a belt

around your

expanding aging waistline

you hold on

for the notch

to somehow

give way

and set you free

coming of age

if beauty is in the
eye of the beholder
how can each of us
behold ourselves
beautiful

we become bent over
like a sturdy branch
in gale force winds
like crinoline
we stand
propping up our creased face
with bulbous fingers
manicured nails

we do what we can do
maintain external integrity
the internal has withstood
a loss deeper than a machete
slicing off a head

we have claimed our headdress

our crown glistens

as our toes cover each other

holding on for the next step

in our measured moments

exonerated

perfect

coming of age

perfect

prevention

there's even a magazine

the size of reader's digest

fits in your hand

with a callus

you didn't prevent

when you dug your garden

you cut your nails

to prevent them

from tearing your stockings

you no longer wear

substituting pants instead

not trying to prevent

your feminine touch

with the silk blouse

left outside your trousers

the dental floss

travels with you

as you seek to prevent decay

to allay embarrassing moments

you grow your organic foods

bathe in handmade plant based aromas

season your life with aware people

natural flavors

homegrown clothes and wares

still

you cannot prevent

death

not with mirth

health

mushroom bliss

you

have your legs waxed

your pussy coiffed

your face dermaplaned

to prevent

the onslaught of messy hair

that might get in the way

of a man's preference

what about

what you prefer

to prevent

essentials

neither wallet

nor purse

pen

or pad

no gas car

instead a plug in

maybe homeless

outfit a super van

run a business

from a local starbucks

we've moved forward

faster mightier

than a stagecoach

even a horse

a novel language

called texting

advanced

greater than

the phoenicians

we are paving a way

for the unknown to rule

and what to say

no handshake made

nor eye contact

displayed

a few measly words

no oxford to spell

sound bytes enough

bank on nothing

bitcoin

on the way

i'll be out

by then

you my friend

are of the new world

maybe a fantastic time

or a very scary place

following disease

smooth out the crinkles

tuck in your shirt

partially

that's in vogue

if these thoughtful moves

matter

no one sees you

you see you

as you think you look

others see themselves

and you

your silver wispy strands

golden flecks

not frosted you claim

it matters

you crane to straighten

your broken back

make your short frame

look elongated

like the imposing figure

on the magazine cover

you're not that age

you're the one

disappearing

except in political office

courtrooms assisted living communes

that age

where your death

is the next big reckoning

along the way

moments of a smile

a tear of belonging

a cooing with your dog

fullness aloneness

a pause of silence

a space for love

INFATUATION

simplistic

infatuation

like a meteor

becomes a crater

infatuation

infatuation

at first it's like a relentless new feeling

takes me to my knees

has me flying

before longing strikes

a word satiates me

next he requests a poem

he's become accustomed

to my making a fuss over him

thinking i fancy him

what does he know about love

and about me

showing him attention with a verse

i express my mirth in words big enough

to catch him off guard

having him question his capacity

to lasso a woman

who goes from fiery to icy

can this southern gentleman

keep priming the pump

or must he capitulate

go home and text me from his truck

will his being in touch

trump this woman's pithy ways

and will he be able to reel her in

just enough to show her

he's her mainstay

what will it take to settle her down

shed her ego or false dreams

to awaken in his arms

to know it's as real as it seems

not on match.com

a wishin'

a hopin'

he would return

from wrestling

the bad guy

his exotic travels

deliver silk wares

rare jewels to bedazzle

lotions potions

to adorn the warm drawn waters

in my claw foot tub

his holster

lays aback

the weaved chair

creased boots beside

his dust brimmed hat

fits the ladder back knob

he's reliably returned

to me

only me

wearing his badge

of ubiquitous honor

i willingly

let him fill my tub

he easily sturdily

steps in

sliding down

i take the brush

he's bought from afar

and scrub his rigid

sturdy back

only he

makes the guns

smoke

he is indeed

my gunsmoke

hyacinth

i had her repeat her name

not for her exquisite accent

i couldn't fathom such a flower

for her identity

hyancinths

a complete smell

three colors to choose

like buying spring heels

to match an easter dress

come to find out

she has a shoe fetish

the higher the heel

the greater the desire

expectedly she does yoga

and wants to practice

with me

she's here to meet

her new in-laws

stunningly attractive

she is the flower incarnate

her lips eggplant

nails popsicle red

hair bouncy brown

eyes and skin to match

a smile

whiter than milk

she existed

everywhere

anywhere

truly cosmopolitan

extraordinaire

she's at home

sitting among japanese

eating with those in poverty

meeting film industry tycoons

or passing a peace pipe in a tepee

my days are over

to be this strong

bold

lovely

fresh

with life ahead of her

she

a bouquet

of hyacinths

for her

upcoming

wedding day

ORDINARY THINGS

the potholder

oh how it would be

to be a potholder

so useful

kept neatly in a drawer

in between a dishtowel

and a ziploc

sometimes front and center

others hanging from its own bespoke hook

maybe permanently soiled

with a burnt spot there

instead of on me

acknowledge it as necessary

offers simple protection

to care for myself

if i could be this useful

ordinary

she hurriedly texted

with both thumbs

i was envious

not that she was connected

instead her simultaneous use

of both thumbs

a library book

rested in her lap

married

two children

photos she showed

in between texting

their joy

tied them together

a bow on a package

loosening

as age split them apart

mom with her hot rolled hair

banana blonde

and body hips wide

from childbirth

next to me

on the short flight

an arm rest

the designated

do not trespass

but i did

and she allowed

i wanted to know

her story

to witness

the package

next to me

unwrap it

to see

happiness

or tragedy

the formula

for either

and what

was in between

what made it

all work

she told me

neither shrills

nor thrills

it all works

because

it's ordinary

outer garment

the nun in her habit
curious in all that garb

all of us
dressed in our habits

patterned energies
steeped often
in falsehoods

we believe
these to be true

we wear them
not calling it armor

a prophylactic
for the heart

remove the habit
and the mirror
is your neighbor

lotus

dressed

curly bound

if sheared

a mat for your tub

a lap warmer to rest

she wears her coat

every season

raincoat in wet

sweater for cool

nightie too

self-adjust temp

repels dander

silky surface

i search for a zipper

underneath and around

none to be found

mine is stuck

catching my skin

can't go forward

or take back steps

my heart sobs

i look for blood stain

dried on the zipper

barely breathing

i poke out my head

the world is cold

i want her coat

westinghouse washer

lift the lid

empty inside

ready to make clean

dirty

the mop head

clanks

next all the rags

used to clear the dust

make clean

dirty

press the buttons

all on go

halts abruptly

interruptions

turbulence

discombobulating

inside

to make clean

dirty

rearrange the pieces

back to the beginning

press the buttons

the lid falls soundfully

the rocking stops

the noise silent

the work

begins

make clean

dirty

plum

a single syllable

easy to form your lips

eggplant colored

or mottled red tones

partake a plum

a succulent choice

the syrupy juice

quenches your deep thirst

for sweetness

in that moment

if you are not distracted

this simple piece of fruit

becomes lusciously extraordinary

ABOUT THE AUTHOR

writing was like my doll, always with me. a worn pocket dictionary, legal pad and fountain pen were my guaranteed companions, my guaranteed playmate.

once school age, i turned my bedroom into an imaginary, though clearly to me, real classroom, where the homespun pillows on my window seat became my students with actual names. and the subject matter was my assigned homework, to complete and study. in the process, i became my own teacher and was able to participate and bring knowledge to others.

when i write, i'm like a thin sliver of a thread in a needle, difficult to insert yet once done, with the perfect end knot secured, the trance begins and all that is torn becomes seamless, sealed, healed and protected.

when my poetry comes to me, i go to a place where nothing else exists, just that sweet moment when the words, like a stream of water, flow, until the sensory valve automatically, with its self-timer, shuts off. i cannot go back and turn it on. It must happen again expressly. i don't have to wait for that moment. i know it will come again and again.

ACKNOWLEDGEMENTS

This small book is an amalgamation and sincere expression of my inward journey, my personal struggle with depression and relentless quest for equanimity and peace.

It began with my first Iyengar yoga class, to an unstoppable commitment for teacher certification at an ashram in Palampur, India. There I was exposed to the Dalai Lama's teachings. A Buddhist friend, Yvonne Mellema, shepherded me to the Dalai Lama's residence time and time again. I will never forget one teaching in particular on how to meditate using a candle flame. It was one of the more remarkable, influential and impactful experiences. From those lectures the trajectory expanded to mindfulness workshops throughout the country. I was fortunate enough to learn from some of the current most powerful Buddhist teachers, leaders and authors. Perhaps the more life altering was with the well-known Buddhist poet, Jane Hirshfield.

I am indebted to my former book editor, Karla Olson, who encouraged me to pursue my poetry, guiding me to my relentlessly patient, compassionate mentor, gentle critic, and publisher, Cornelia Feye.

I attempt to remain a student in all my endeavors, never feeling like I know; instead, I allow and listen for the lessons that serve to illuminate my inner voice, to hear that vibration that channels through me, becoming my free form poetic expressions.

This book is about my suffering and thirst for sanity, peace, levity, and connection. My hope is that you find empathy, identification, and connection, that you can hold these words up close as a friend to console you on your journey, to know you are not alone, different, or strange. You belong and it's okay.

All proceeds go to NIMH, the National Institute of Mental Health.

Botanical Illustrations by Irina Gronborg

TENDERNESS   tulip

CONNECTION   protea

DISCONNECTION   nasturtium

SENSUALITY   epiphyllums

DOUBT   bean sprouts

SENSIBILITY   trumpet vine

DARKNESS   tillandsia

INSIGHT   altissima rose

SUFFERING   graptopetalum

BECOMING   morning glory

INFATUATION   Betty Boop Rose

ORDINARY THINGS   tulip bouquet

Made in the USA
Monee, IL
25 February 2022

91847097R00111